THE PHARAOH'S COURT

LIFE IN ANCIENT EGYPT

THE PHARAOH'S COURT

BY

KATHRYN HINDS

Marshall Cavendish
Benchmark
New York

To Mom and Dad
for all the times you took me to the library to get books about ancient Egypt

The author and publisher wish to specially thank J. Brett McClain of the Oriental Institute of the University of Chicago for his invaluable help in reviewing the manuscript.

MARSHALL CAVENDISH BENCHMARK 99 WHITE PLAINS ROAD TARRYTOWN, NEW YORK 10591-9001
www.marshallcavendish.us

LIBRARY OF CONGRESS CATALOGING-IN-PUBLICATION DATA: Hinds, Kathryn, 1962-   The pharaoh's court / by Kathryn Hinds.-- 1st ed.   p. cm. -- (Life in ancient Egypt)   Summary: "Describes the daily life of the upper classes during the New Kingdom period of ancient Egypt, from about 1550 BCE to about 1070 BCE, including the structure of society, the differing roles of men and women, and what it was like to be a child in that era"--Provided by publisher.   Includes bibliographical references and index.   ISBN-13: 978-0-7614-2183-2 ISBN-10: 0-7614-2183-1   1. Egypt--Court and courtiers--Juvenile literature. 2. Egypt--Social life and customs--To 332 B.C.--Juvenile literature. I. Title. II. Series. DT61.H48 2006   932'.014--dc22   2005027941

EDITOR: Joyce Stanton   EDITORIAL DIRECTOR: Michelle Bisson
ART DIRECTOR: Anahid Hamparian   SERIES DESIGNER: Michael Nelson

Images provided by Rose Corbett Gordon, Art Editor, Mystic CT, from the following sources: cover: The Art Archive/Egyptian Museum Cairo/Dagli Orti; back cover: Luxor Museum, Egypt/Scala/Art Resource, NY; page i: Ashmolean Museum, University of Oxford/Bridgeman Art Library; pages iii, 26, 35, 37, 40, 55, 58, 61, 62: Erich Lessing/Art Resource, NY; pages vi, 39, 48: Werner Forman/Art Resource, NY; page viii: Scala/Art Resource, NY; pages 2, 14: The Art Archive/Egyptian Museum Cairo/Dagli Orti; pages 3, 13: Gianni Dagli Orti/Corbis; page 7: The Art Archive/Musée du Louvre/Dagli Orti; pages 9, 19, 43: The Art Archive/Dagli Orti; pages 10, 56: The Art Archive/British Museum/Dagli Orti; pages 15, 63: Werner Forman/Corbis; page 17: Mary Evans Picture Library/Guy Lyon Playfair; page 18: British Museum/Bridgeman Art Library; page 20: The Art Archive/Egyptian Museum Turin/Dagli Orti; page 23: Luxor Museum, Egypt/Scala/Art Resource, NY; page 25: Mary Evans Picture Library; page 27: The Art Archive/Luxor Museum, Egypt/Dagli Orti; page 29: The Stapleton Collection/Bridgeman Art Library; page 30: Christel Gerstenberg/Corbis; pages 32, 33, 38: Aegyptisches Museum/Bildarchiv Preussischer Kulturbesitz/ Art Resource, NY; page 42: The Art Archive/Ragab Papyrus Institute Cairo/Dagli Orti; page 45: Saqqara, Egypt, Ancient Art and Architecture Collection Ltd./Bridgeman Art Library; page 46: Egyptian National Museum, Cairo/Bridgeman Art Library; page 51: Valley of the Nobles, Thebes, Egypt/Giraudon/Bridgeman Art Library; page 52: Holton Collection/SuperStock; page 53: age fotostock/SuperStock.

Printed in China
3 5 6 4 2

front cover: Tutankhamen and his wife, Ankhesenamen, portrayed on the backrest of his throne
half-title page: Pharaoh Thutmose I
title page: A government official and his wife listen to a harpist.
page vi: The wife of a government official, holding a bouquet of lotus flowers
back cover: A group of New Kingdom scribes

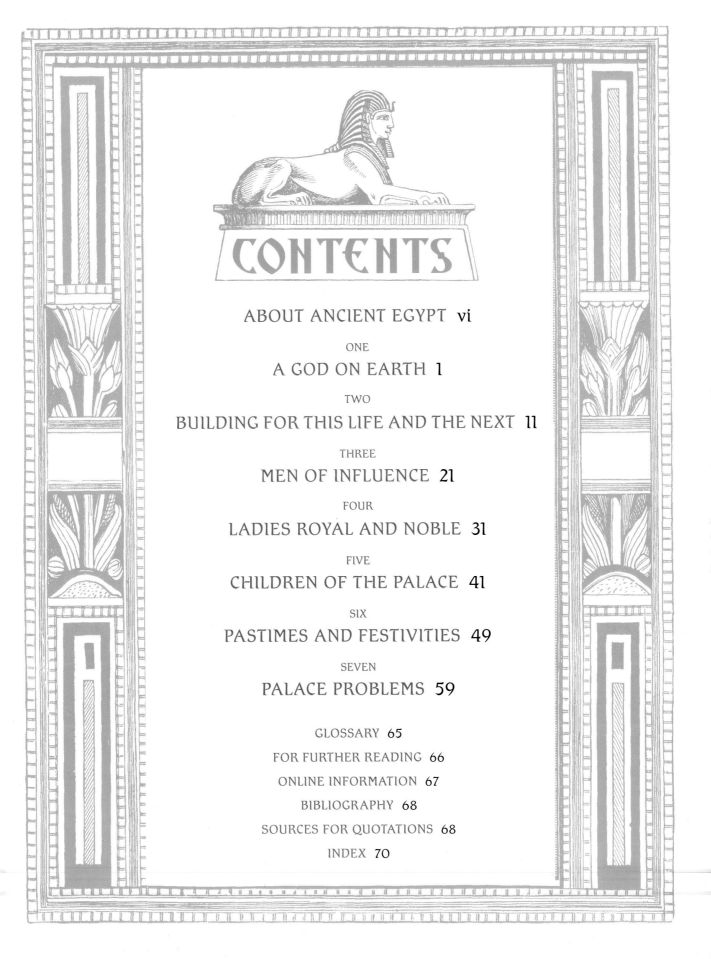

CONTENTS

ABOUT ANCIENT EGYPT

When we think about ancient Egypt, magnificent images immediately come to mind: the pyramids, the Sphinx, the golden funeral mask of "King Tut," colossal statues of mighty kings. Our imaginations are full of mummies and tombs, hieroglyphic symbols and animal-headed goddesses and gods. Most of us, however, don't often give much thought to the people of ancient Egypt and how they lived their everyday lives. Where would we even start?

Ancient Egyptian history is vast—about three thousand years long, in fact, from the first known pharaoh (Aha, also called Menes) to the last independent ruler (Cleopatra VII). During this span of time, Egyptian society and culture naturally underwent many changes. So to make it easier to get to know the people of ancient Egypt, this series of books focuses on a smaller chunk of history, the period known as the New Kingdom, from about 1550 to about 1070 BCE. This was the era of ancient Egypt's greatest power and the time of some of its most famous pharaohs, or rulers: Hatshepsut, Thutmose III, Amenhotep III, Akhenaten, Tutankhamen, Ramses II.

During the New Kingdom, Egypt was the dominant force in the

Mediterranean world—a true superpower. The pharaohs controlled territory from Syria to what is now Sudan, and their influence stretched to Asia Minor and Mesopotamia. Yet no matter how wide their connections, the Egyptians maintained a unique culture with its own writing, artistic style, religion, type of government, and social organization. And always at the center of life was the Nile River, which made Egypt a long, narrow oasis of fertile greenery in the midst of the desert.

In this book you will meet people at the top level of Egyptian society—kings, queens, royal children, nobles—and some of the scribes, generals, servants, and entertainers who surrounded them. You will visit palaces, temples, and tombs. You will learn how aristocratic Egyptians relaxed, and you will also see some of the hardships they suffered. So step back into history, to a time even before the splendors of ancient Greece and Rome. Welcome to life in ancient Egypt!

A variety of systems of dating have been used by different cultures throughout history. Many historians now prefer to use BCE (Before Common Era) and CE (Common Era) instead of BC (Before Christ) and AD (Anno Domini), out of respect for the diversity of the world's peoples.

ONE

A GOD ON EARTH

The Egyptian pharaoh was more than a king. His power was immense: he was the head of the government, the army, and the priesthood. In theory, at least, he owned all of the country's land and its resources. After death he would be acknowledged as a god, worshipped by people at all levels of society. During the New Kingdom, it became more and more common for the pharaoh to be regarded as divine even during his lifetime.

Thutmose I (1504–1492 BCE) left inscriptions asserting that the mighty god Amen was his father—and as the son of a god, Thutmose must also be divine. Thutmose's successors, including the female pharaoh Hatshepsut, didn't hesitate to make the same claim. It was Ramses II, however, more than two hundred years after Thutmose, who really embraced earthly godhood. By the eighth year of his reign, he had a gigantic statue of himself carved and named Ramses-the-god. It was the first of many such statues, all over Egypt,

Opposite:
Pharaoh Thutmose III kneels to make offerings to the gods.

In this scene symbolizing Egypt's supremacy over its neighbors, Ramses II grasps a Nubian, a Libyan, and a Syrian by their hair. The ceremonial ax in the pharaoh's hand is a symbol of his divine power.

that became the focus of worship. There are even wall carvings that show Ramses himself making offerings to Ramses-the-god.

Having a god for a king reinforced the Egyptians' belief that their nation was supreme on Earth. It seemed Egypt's destiny to rule, as Thutmose I claimed, "all that the sun disc encircled."

WARRIOR-KINGS

The first New Kingdom pharaoh, Ahmose (1550–1525 BCE), began his career as ruler over southern Egypt only. For a hundred years, the north had been in the hands of people known as the Hyksos, or "Foreign Princes," originally from lands in western Asia. Ahmose's father and older brother had both tried to drive out the Hyksos, but it was Ahmose who at last succeeded. His mastery of new military techniques, centered on the use of chariots and archers, made him a force to be reckoned with. Not only did he reunify northern and southern Egypt under his rule, but he began to extend Egyptian power south into Nubia (modern-day Sudan) and east into Asia.

Ahmose's achievements set the pattern for the pharaohs that followed him. For generations to come, the ideal Egyptian ruler would be a brave warrior—a conqueror, a winner of victories—who personally led troops in battle. "His majesty became enraged like a leopard. His majesty shot and his first arrow pierced the chest of that foe." This description of Thutmose I's activities on the battlefield in Nubia is typical of the praise given to Egypt's warrior-kings. And during the New Kingdom period, there were a lot of battles to fight. Some were necessary to protect Egypt's borders, especially in the east. But the pharaohs were ambitious, too. Eventually, secure borders weren't enough, and Egypt embarked on wars of conquest.

The most successful of the warrior-pharaohs was probably Thutmose III (1479–1425), sometimes referred to as "the Napoleon of ancient Egypt." Like that other famous conqueror, Thutmose was short (even by ancient standards)—just five feet tall. There was nothing small about his abilities, however. Not long after coming to power, he set off to the northeast at the head of his army. He was retracing the steps of his grandfather, Thutmose I, who had previously pushed Egyptian influence as far as northern Syria. But in recent years, the Syrians had been getting restless and rebellious, threatening Egypt's trade routes and its power.

Thutmose III, wearing a ceremonial false beard and the crown of Osiris, the god with whom kings were identified after they died

Thutmose III's major battle of this first campaign was outside the walls of Megiddo, in what is now Israel. According to an inscription in the great temple of Amen at Karnak, when the Egyptian forces made their advance, the city's defenders "fled headlong to Megiddo in terror, abandoning their horses and their chariots

HITTITE EMPIRE

GREECE

ASIA MINOR
(ANATOLIA)

MITANNI

TIGRIS RIVER

MESOPOTAMIA

EUPHRATES RIVER

SYRIA
LEBANON

MEDITERRANEAN SEA

Megiddo

JORDAN RIVER

Babylon

NILE DELTA

LIBYA

LOWER EGYPT

Giza
Saqqara Memphis

SINAI

EGYPT

SAHARA

NILE RIVER

UPPER EGYPT

EGYPT
AND ITS NEIGHBORS
DURING THE
NEW KINGDOM

N
W   E
S

Valley of the Kings Thebes

RED SEA

NUBIA

Abu Simbel

EGYPTIAN–RULED
TERRITORY
IN THE 1400s BCE

MILES

0   100   200

of gold and silver, and the people hauled them up into the city, pulling them by their clothing." Thutmose then besieged the city; faced with starvation, the inhabitants finally yielded. The Egyptians took everything of value, but Thutmose did show some mercy to Megiddo's allies; in another inscription, he said, "Then my Majesty gave them leave to go to their towns. They all went by donkey, so that I might take their horses."

By the time this campaign was over, Thutmose had swept all the way up through the Lebanon region. The next year he was on the march again, and so it went, until he had Syria firmly under control. Then he faced his greatest foe, the empire of Mitanni, in the region of the upper Euphrates River. By this time Thutmose's reputation was so great that the king of Mitanni fled without giving battle, leaving his country open to the Egyptian forces. This confirmed Egypt's position as the superpower of the eastern Mediterranean. Thutmose made sure it stayed that way. In all he led about seventeen military campaigns, in which more than 350 cities fell to him. His victories brought Egypt undreamed-of wealth and power.

MAINTAINING THE COSMIC ORDER

The best-known symbol of ancient Egypt is probably the pyramid. This is fitting in more ways than one, for the Egyptian social structure can be pictured as a pyramid. At the bottom were the workers and farmers, the vast majority of the people. Next came artisans, specialists in various crafts. These craftspeople, like the farmers and laborers, were supervised by the overseers and foremen on the next level. Above them were village mayors. A still smaller number of people made up the rank above, that of army officers, courtiers, and provincial governors. Just below the peak of the pyramid were the pharaoh's closest friends and advisers. At the very top, of course, was the pharaoh himself.

Like the pyramid, this social order was pretty much set in stone. It was how things were, how they were fated to be. Talent and connections sometimes enabled individuals to climb higher on the pyramid. But whatever rank you held, you knew your place. You knew how you were supposed to act within your social class and how you were to behave to those both higher and lower than you. This was all part of *maat,* the proper, divinely intended order of the universe. The alternative to order was chaos, which the Egyptians dreaded above all things. And so the pharaoh, from his position at the summit of the pyramid, had the responsibility, first and foremost, of preserving *maat.*

The pharaoh's military activities were one way of fulfilling this role, since it was seen as an offense against *maat* for any part of Egypt to fall under foreign rule, or even for another country to rival Egypt's power. The pharaoh also had religious duties that helped maintain *maat*: every day he was expected to go into the most sacred and secret part of the temple of Amen to pray and make offerings on behalf of the nation. As the main link between Egypt and the divine realm, the pharaoh was regarded as chief priest not only of Amen, but of all the gods; all other priests were simply his deputies.

Maat means not only "order" but also "truth" and "justice." Archaeologists have not yet found any written law code from the New Kingdom, but we do have inscriptions that record pharaohs' occasional decrees about various crimes and their punishments. In a sense, the pharaoh himself embodied the law. Because he shared in the divine nature of the gods, he was trusted to understand and interpret the requirements of *maat*. This trust extended to anyone whom he deputized to hear cases and make judgments on his behalf. The *Instruction for Merikare,* written for an earlier prince but still well known in the New Kingdom, sets down the basic guidelines for administering justice:

Syrian and Nubian captives pay homage to Horemheb, who was a general under Tutankhamen and eventually became the last pharaoh of the Eighteenth Dynasty.

Act justly, that you may endure on earth. Quieten him who weeps; do not dispossess the widow; do not deprive a man of his father's property. Do not put down high officials from their offices. Avoid punishing wrongfully. Do not smite (anyone) with the knife: there is no profit in it for you. You should punish by beating and imprisonment—in this way will the whole land be ordered—except for the rebel whose plans have been discovered.

Rebellion against the pharaoh was one of the worst possible offenses against *maat*. The Egyptians often regarded enemy leaders as nothing more than rebels, but there seem to be very few instances of Egyptians themselves attempting to overthrow their ruler. Once a pharaoh was crowned, his person was sacred. He himself—his very existence—was necessary for the preservation of *maat*. Without him, there was only chaos.

A NOTE ON DATES, DYNASTIES, AND NAMES

The dates of the pharaohs' reigns and the spelling of their names used in this book generally follow *The Oxford History of Ancient Egypt*, edited by Ian Shaw. However, if you continue to study ancient Egypt, you will see other dates and other spellings. Here's why:

The ancient Egyptians did not calculate dates by numbering the years from a single fixed starting point as we do. Instead, they numbered the years from the beginning of each pharaoh's reign. For example, they would record events as taking place in the second year of the reign of Tutankhamen or the tenth year of the reign of Horemheb. It is often difficult to convert Egyptian dates to our dating system, so various sources give differing dates for the events of ancient Egyptian history. For this reason, all dates in this book must be considered approximate.

Scholars have traditionally divided the three thousand years of ancient Egyptian history into the following eras: the Early Dynastic Period, the Old Kingdom, the First Intermediate Period, the Middle Kingdom, the Second Intermediate Period, the New Kingdom, the Third Intermediate Period, the Late Period, and the Greco-Roman Period. The New Kingdom was comprised of three dynasties: the Eighteenth (1550–1295 BCE), Nineteenth (1295–1186 BCE), and Twentieth (1186–1069 BCE). The Eighteenth Dynasty occupies roughly the middle of ancient Egypt's history as an independent nation.

As for names, the ancient Egyptian language poses a unique set of problems. Scholars have been able to read Egyptian hieroglyphs—the famous pictures signs of ancient Egypt—since 1822. But most hieroglyphs did not stand for individual letters and their sounds, as in our alphabet. A few hieroglyphs represented single consonants, but most of them stood for groups of consonants or for entire words or concepts. Vowels were rarely indicated. These facts have made it a challenge for Egyptologists to decide on the best way to use our alphabet to spell ancient Egyptian names and words. Different spellings have been preferred at different times and places, and even today there is no agreement among scholars on exact spellings.

Hieroglyphs are incorporated into this tomb painting of an official and his wife.

TWO

BUILDING FOR THIS LIFE AND THE NEXT

gypt has often been called "the gift of the Nile," and the ancient Egyptians would certainly have agreed with this nickname. There is almost no rainfall in Egypt, so the river has always been the country's major source of water. The Nile gave Egypt the gift of life in another way, too: every year it flooded, depositing a layer of silt on both riverbanks. This silt constantly renewed Egypt's soil, making the Nile Valley one of the most fertile regions in the ancient world. Because of the richness of the soil, the Egyptians called their country Kemet, "The Black Land"—contrasting it with the surrounding desert, known as the Red Land.

In the Nile Valley, the Black Land was only about ten miles wide—less in some places. The Egyptians cherished this narrow strip of fertile land and reserved as much as possible for farming. They built their villages, towns, palaces, and temples on raised ground near the riverbank, or at the edge of the farmland, where it gave way to desert. The desert itself, with the cliffs that rose beyond it, was the realm of the dead.

Opposite:
The Nile supported a rich ecosystem, as can be seen in this painting of a nobleman and his family enjoying a day of hunting waterfowl in the marshes.

ROYAL RESIDENCES

Nile mud was a valuable resource not only for farmers, but also for builders: sun-dried mud brick was the most common construction material in ancient Egypt. It was so easy to make and to use that even palaces and noblemen's villas were built of it. The drawback of mud brick, however, is that it is not a lasting material. For this reason there are few remains of ancient Egyptian homes—even those of the most powerful and wealthy. Luckily, Egyptologists have been able to piece together quite a bit of information from the surviving evidence.

One of the most important buildings in Egypt was, of course, the pharaoh's palace. It was more than just a home for him and his family—it was at the heart of government administration. There the pharaoh sat in judgment, received foreign diplomats, issued instructions to his officials, and dictated to his scribes. In fact, since the pharaoh himself *was* the government of Egypt, he had palaces up and down the Nile so that wherever he was, he could conduct the business of ruling the country.

There was no standard design for royal palaces, but each seems to have had three important elements: one or more throne rooms; a large, columned hall; and a Window of Appearance. This was a fairly large rectangular opening, perhaps with a balcony, where the pharaoh could show himself to his people or watch religious processions and other spectacles. When the pharaoh wanted to reward a loyal official or brave general, he held a public ceremony at the Window of Appearance: those he was honoring stood below the Window, and he reached out and awarded them gold collars or necklaces called the Gold of Praise.

Palaces also had suites of rooms for the personal use of the pharaoh and his family. A typical suite might have a bedroom, a robing room, a storeroom, a bathroom, and perhaps a parlor or sit-

An artist's reconstruction of a courtyard inside an Egyptian palace

ting room. During most of the New Kingdom, the queen and other royal women had their own suites—sometimes even their own palaces—separate from the king's.

Other palace amenities included courtyards and gardens, usually ornamented by pools or ponds; offices; stables; kitchens; and storage areas, often including warehouses for grain. Amenhotep III's ceremonial palace near Thebes formed such a large compound that it was like a small city. There were four palace buildings, a festival hall, an artificial lake for boat-borne processions, a temple, chapels, houses for the highest-ranking courtiers, cottages for lesser officials, servants' quarters, workshops, and even a village for workers and craftspeople. The whole sprawling complex was connected to the Nile by a canal, so the king and his court could easily leave and return by boat as needed.

LUXURIOUS LIVING

Palace walls were as much as twelve feet thick to help keep out the heat. For the same reason, windows were narrow and placed high on the wall. Alabaster oil lamps, often intricately crafted, provided artificial light when necessary, illuminating the beauties of the palace interior. The walls were whitewashed and then painted with murals in vivid colors. The most popular wall decorations seem to have been scenes from nature; sometimes they adorned painted floors as well.

Royal Egyptians, it seems, did not clutter their palaces with a lot of furniture—but what they had was, naturally, of the best quality. Valuable imported woods, such as ebony and cedar, were often used, and artists added decoration in the form of carving, painting, gilding, or inlays of glass, ivory, colored wood, and semiprecious stone. One of the most famous pieces of ancient Egyptian furniture, a throne of Tutankhamen, shows a number of these techniques.

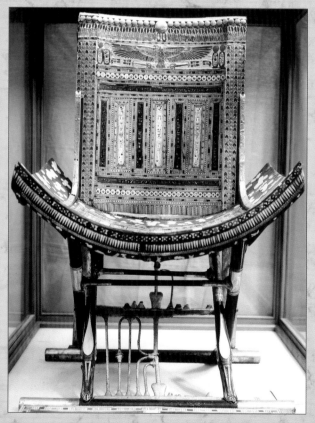

Furniture included chairs, with or without arms, some with short legs; stools; small tables; wooden storage chests; and beds. The Egyptian bed was uniquely designed: it had a slight downward slant, so while there was no headboard, there was always a footboard to prevent the sleeper from sliding out of bed. No mattresses or pillows were used—they probably would have been uncomfortable in Egypt's hot climate. Instead of a mat-

One of the exquisitely crafted thrones buried with Tutankhamen

tress, there was a pad of folded linen; instead of a pillow, there was a shoulder-height wooden headrest.

Storeroom shelves held baskets, wooden chests, pottery and alabaster jars, and glass bottles—a variety of containers for a variety of royal possessions. These included luxurious personal-care items such as jars or bottles of perfumed oil, polished bronze mirrors in special carrying bags, and chests full of cosmetics (which were used by men and women alike). There might also have been wooden mannequins, to hold and display wigs and large, jeweled collars.

The lid of a wooden storage chest, inlaid with ivory and other materials to portray Tutankhamen and his queen in a garden

The bathroom featured a slab of limestone on the floor in the corner, with additional limestone against the walls to protect them from water. A bather stood on this stone floor while servants poured jars of water over him or her; the water drained out through a spout at one side. Close to this room was often another room, provided with a stone or wooden toilet seat held up by bricks; under the seat there would have been a pottery jar or perhaps a box of sand. The Egyptians also had portable toilet stools, designed to hold a container underneath a wooden seat with a hole in it.

MIGHTY MONUMENTS

Pharaohs built their palaces for the practical purposes of living and governing, not to impress future generations. But every king wanted his name to be remembered, by both the gods and the people of Egypt, for all time. Sometimes when we want to emphasize the permanence or importance of something, we say it's "carved in stone." And having their names and deeds carved into great stone monuments was the pharaohs' favorite way of leaving a lasting impression.

The most honored god among the New Kingdom pharaohs was Amen. The center of his worship was at Thebes, where the temple of Karnak was dedicated to him. It was a tradition for successive pharaohs to add to this temple, showing ever greater devotion to the god. Amenhotep I (1525–1504) added a number of shrines and chapels, as well as a pylon, a kind of gigantic gateway. Thutmose I lengthened the processional ways leading to the temple; added two more pylons and a large, columned hall; and also contributed two obelisks. These tall, four-sided columns, with their pyramid-shaped tips covered in gold foil, symbolized the rays of the sun. Thutmose I's daughter, Hatshepsut, had two more pairs of obelisks added to the temple, as well as another pylon and a red granite chapel. And so it went.

Pharaohs did not concentrate all their efforts on the Karnak temple—they built temples throughout Egypt, to many different gods. Some rulers also made a point of restoring monuments from the Old and Middle Kingdoms. Thutmose IV (1400–1390) even conducted what might have been the world's first example of "rescue archaeology." As he told it himself, one day he was out hunting near the Sphinx, until he grew tired:

> He relaxed in the shadow of this great god and sleep
> overcame him just at the time that the sun was at its

height. Then he discovered the Majesty of this Great God was speaking out of his very own mouth, just as a father addresses his son, saying, "Look at me, gaze at me, my own son. . . . My state is that of one in trouble . . . and the desert sand is covering the place in which I sit. I have waited to have you carry out that which is in my heart for I know you, saying, 'You are my son and my protector. . . .'"

Thutmose's dream convinced him to order the clearing away of the sand that had buried the lower portions of the Sphinx, which was at this point over a thousand years old. Thutmose recorded his deed on a stela, or stone plaque, set up between the Sphinx's paws.

Indeed, the pharaohs looked at any stone monument as an ideal place to record and immortalize their deeds. The walls of temples, the sides of pylons and obelisks, the bases of colossal statues—all were covered with carved hieroglyphs and pictures glorifying the pharaohs and the gods. The monuments themselves demonstrated the pharaoh's, and therefore Egypt's, power and prosperity—evidence that reassured the people that *maat* was being upheld.

HOUSES OF ETERNITY

The pharaoh was important to Egypt not only in life but also in death, for then he joined the company of the gods, the country's divine guardians. According to Egyptian

The ruins of the Karnak temple around 1850. One of the obelisks can be seen, still standing, in the background.

belief, however, the soul could not survive if the body was destroyed. This is why mummification developed into such a high art. It was thought that a body preserved as a mummy could last forever. Indeed, a number of them have survived for thousands of years so far, some in such excellent condition that we can even examine ancient hairstyles.

As the living pharaoh had his "great house," or palace, so the dead pharaoh had his "house of eternity"—his tomb. Here his mummy was laid to rest, accompanied by a large number and variety of his possessions. Since the afterlife was thought of as a perfected version of this life, everything that the pharaoh might find useful or enjoyable was buried with him. If the actual item couldn't be included for some reason, a picture or model of it would do—art had a magical quality that could make the things depicted become real (in the right circumstances, at least). Words had a similar power. Objects in the tomb, and the tomb walls, were covered with hieroglyphs that gave the dead pharaoh the keys to a successful afterlife.

In this tomb painting, priests support mummies while women mourn.

Paintings also embellished tomb walls, with scenes of death and the afterlife and also images to remind the deceased of the joys of living. The ceiling was sometimes decorated with paintings of stars and constellations.*

Early in the New Kingdom, it became the custom to build royal tombs in the western desert across the Nile from Thebes. This cemetery,

* More information on mummies and Egyptian beliefs about the afterlife can be found in another book in this series, *Life in Ancient Egypt: Religion*.

which the Egyptians called the Great Place, has come to be known as the Valley of the Kings. The many-chambered tombs were dug deep into the solid rock of the desert cliffs. The location of a pharaoh's tomb was kept secret from everyone except the workers and the trusted advisers who oversaw the labor. Amenhotep I's faithful overseer of building projects, Ineni, recorded that he "supervised the excavation of the cliff-tomb of His Majesty alone, no one seeing, no one hearing."

A portion of the Valley of the Kings. In the foreground can be seen the entrances to the tombs of Seti I and Ramses I.

Although the house of eternity was not meant to be seen by the public, the pharaoh still needed a place where his family and others could come to make offerings and pray to his spirit. This purpose was served by buildings known as mortuary temples, which were constructed at some distance from the tomb and close to the edge of the farmland. Incredible effort was lavished on mortuary temples. Amenhotep III, for example, described his as "a fortress made out of fine white sandstone, wrought entirely with gold, its floors decorated with silver and all of its doors decorated with electrum . . . Its lake was filled by the high Nile, possessor of fish and ducks, and brightened with baskets of flowers. Its workshops were filled with male and female servants." The only parts of this structure that survive today, however, are two gigantic statues of Amenhotep III, seated on his throne; they have come to be known as the Colossi of Memnon and have attracted tourists since Roman times.

THREE

MEN OF INFLUENCE

 o pharaoh, no matter how powerful, could rule Egypt entirely alone. It was vital that he have a group of trusted administrators to whom he could delegate authority. Even on the rare occasions when the pharaoh was a woman, these government ministers were always men. Quite often they were relatives or close friends of the king. He paid them a handsome salary, which he supplemented with gifts. These high officials also had the right to receive land rents and, from time to time, shares in the revenue taken in by Egypt's temples. The pharaoh further rewarded his faithful deputies by giving them their own rock-cut tombs.

Like all Egyptians, officials of every rank were expected to conduct themselves according to *maat*: with honesty, fairness, understanding, respect to their superiors, and charity and kindliness toward the weak and poor. This ideal was summed up by the vizier Rekhmire, in these words on one of the walls of his tomb:

Opposite:
The vizier Neferrenpet, who served one of the kings of the Nineteenth Dynasty

21

I judged both [the insignificant] and the influential; I rescued the weak man from the strong man; I deflected the fury of the evil man and subdued the greedy man. . . . I succoured the widow who has no husband; I established the son and heir on the seat of his father. I gave [bread to the hungry], water to the thirsty, and meat, oil and clothes to him who had nothing. . . . I never took a bribe from anyone.

THE PHARAOH'S RIGHT-HAND MAN

The highest government appointment was that of vizier (also spelled *vizir*)—a kind of prime minister. There were two viziers, one based in the city of Memphis, close to the Nile Delta, who had responsibility for northern Egypt. The other lived in Thebes and was responsible for southern Egypt. In the New Kingdom the Theban vizier was, it seems, the most powerful of the two, largely because of the great religious and ceremonial importance of his headquarters city.

A vizier was sworn in with great solemnity in front of the entire court, gathered in the king's audience chamber. The ceremony began with the pharaoh exhorting his new official: "See to the office of vizier; be watchful over everything done in it. . . . For it is the support of the whole land." He went on to instruct the vizier to act in justice and fairness: "See equally the man you know and the man you do not know, the man who is near you and the man who is far away. . . . Do not dismiss a petitioner before you have considered his words. . . . Do not lose your temper improperly. . . . The worth of a magistrate comes through behaving justly."

A major part of the vizier's duties was to administer justice on the pharaoh's behalf. Local authorities dealt with many legal cases, but the most serious and the most difficult to solve were brought

The vizier commanded a large staff of scribes, like these, to make reports and records for him.

before the vizier. He was expected to base his rulings on earlier decisions made in similar cases, so attached to his courtroom was "a hall with records of all judgements." The king's instructions to the vizier were clear about the importance of referring to these and not relying on his personal opinions: "Do not act as you wish in matters about which the law is known."

The vizier had a great many other responsibilities, and his days were busy. In the morning, at his house, he received reports—on the correct sealing of the royal strong rooms, the conditions of fortresses, the comings and goings at the palace, and other matters. After issuing any necessary instructions, he went to the palace himself, to greet the king and inform him how things stood in the realm. Then the vizier met with the chief treasurer, and they made their daily reports to each other. After his palace business, the vizier returned to his own hall to hear petitioners.

The vizier was entrusted with putting all of the pharaoh's decrees into action. He took care of everything from organizing tax assessments and the distribution of land to arranging for the troops who accompanied the king as he traveled up and down the Nile. A text called *The Duties of the Vizier* even says,

It is he who should dispatch (men) to cut down syco-more trees when it is specified in the King's House. It is he who should dispatch regional officers to construct dykes throughout the whole land. It is he who should dispatch mayors and district governors to (arrange) the cultivation in the summer. It is he who should appoint the overseer of sheriffs in the hall of the King's House.

The vizier accomplished his duties with the help of a huge staff of scribes, messengers, and government agents. He was also the supervisor of other important officials, including the treasurer and the overseer of the royal granaries.

RUNNING THE EMPIRE

The Egyptians thought of their country as the Two Lands, Upper Egypt (the south) and Lower Egypt (the north). The two viziers each had charge of one of these divisions. For more efficient administration, Egypt was also divided into a varying number of provinces, often called nomes. Each had a governor, or nomarch, who reported to the appropriate vizier. Among the governors' most important responsibilities were managing the use of land and water to assure plentiful harvests, and making sure that taxes were collected properly.

The non-Egyptian territories under the pharaoh's rule were governed differently. In the south, Nubia, also known as Kush, was a virtual colony of Egypt during the New Kingdom. It was under the authority of a viceroy, who was of such importance that he held the title King's Son of Kush. A major part of his job was collecting tribute from the Nubians, especially gold. Nubia had other valuable

Ramses II's temple at Abu Simbel in 1909. During the 1960s the construction of a dam on the Nile flooded this site—but an international rescue effort saved the temple, moving it piece by piece to higher ground.

resources, as well as access to parts of Africa with such much-prized products as elephant ivory, giraffe and leopard skins, and incense. The viceroy also oversaw the pharaoh's building projects in Nubia. The greatest of these was Ramses II's temple at Abu Simbel in northern Nubia. Still standing, its front features four statues of the pharaoh, each about sixty-six feet high. The temple took almost twenty years to complete, with the labor of "multitudes of workmen from the captivity of his [Ramses'] sword in every land."

Egypt's northeastern conquests lay in a region of well-established city-states (roughly the area occupied by the modern countries of Israel, Lebanon, and Syria). It was divided into three provinces, with governors who were usually Egyptians. Sometimes, however, they were "Asiatics," as the people of the region were known in Egypt. The governors shared power with local rulers, chiefs, and mayors. These men were left in office so long as they stayed loyal to Egypt and paid their tribute on time. To make extra certain, these local leaders were compelled to send their sons to the pharaoh's court to be educated in Egyptian ways—the boys were hostages in one sense, but they were also being trained to succeed their fathers as loyal vassals of Egypt.

FAVORED BY THE KING

The pharaoh had a large personal staff. Among its leading members were his steward, who managed the royal estates; his chamberlain, who oversaw the running of the palace; and the first herald, whose duties included supervising the palace guard. Serving under these high officials were a variety of lower officials, scribes, pages, accountants, servants, craftspeople, and others, all filling the pharaoh's court and palaces with bustling activity.

Friends, advisers, and family members also attended the king. They were often given elaborate titles, some of which may not have had much relation to specific duties. We have to wonder just what a nobleman referred to as Sandal Bearer of the King did, or if a courtier with the title Royal Washer Man personally handled the pharaoh's laundry. (More likely, he had the important task of supervising the palace laundry, which must have been quite a large operation.) A Fan Bearer on the Right of the King, on the other hand, probably did shade and cool his monarch with an ornate ostrich-feather fan, since

Servants carry elegant ostrich-feather fans in a procession.

this gave him a privileged spot at the pharaoh's side.

Architects seem to have been particularly esteemed members of the royal court. The architect Ineni served Amenhotep I, Thutmose II, and Hatshepsut. Of Thutmose II, he wrote, "I was a favourite of the king in his every place . . . I possessed the favour of His Majesty every day. I was supplied from the table of the king with bread." Thutmose's queen and successor, Hatshepsut, was similarly generous to Ineni: "Her Majesty praised me. She loved me. She recognized my worth at court, she presented me with things, she magnified me, she filled my house with silver and gold, with all beautiful stuffs of the royal house . . . I increased beyond everything." Amenhotep III's chief architect, Amenhotep son of Hapu, received the privilege of placing a statue of himself outside one of the pylons of the Karnak temple of Amen. About a thousand years later, Amenhotep son of Hapu would come to be regarded as a god himself.

Many of the pharaoh's friends and courtiers played multiple roles. Tutankhamen's chief treasurer, Maya, was also the Overseer of the Great Place. A man named Tjanuny was an army commander, a scribe, and, we might even say, a historian in the court of Thutmose III: he had the walls of his tomb inscribed, "I recorded the victories he [the king] won in every land, putting them into writing according to the facts." Hatshepsut's vizier Hapuseneb was also one of her chief architects and the First Prophet, or high priest, of Amen.

The courtier most famous for his multiple roles is probably

The royal architect Amenhotep son of Hapu. This statue is more than three feet high and stood near one of the pylons in the Karnak temple. Amenhotep is portrayed with rolls of fat to show that he has reached a prosperous, successful old age.

Senenmut, who also served Hatshepsut, both before and after she became pharaoh. During the course of his career, he held such varied positions as tutor or guardian to Hatshepsut's daughter, Overseer of Royal Works, Overseer of the Granaries of Amen, Chief Steward of Amen, and several other posts in Amen's temple. Senenmut also bore the interesting titles Superintendent of the Private Apartments, Superintendent of the Royal Bedroom, and Superintendent of the Bathroom. Scholars are not sure what duties went along with these titles. Clearly, though, Senenmut was one of the pharaoh's closest and most valued advisers.

LEADING THE ARMY

The commander in chief of the Egyptian military was, of course, the pharaoh. But not every pharaoh was able to lead the army in every battle. So just as the king had deputies in the government administration, he had deputies in the military. Indeed, a man might hold positions at court, in the government, in the army, and even in religious institutions, all simultaneously. A good example of this is Amenhotep III's father-in-law, Yuya; among his many titles were "the Hereditary Prince, Courtier, . . . praised of the Good God (the King), confidant of the King, . . . Overseer of the Cattle of [the god] Min, Master of the Royal Horses, King's Lieutenant of Chariotry, High Priest of Min."

While some titles held by courtiers were probably just honorary, indicating their closeness to the pharaoh, titles such as Lieutenant of Chariotry were connected to important responsibilities. The Lieutenant of Chariotry had command of the army's elite troops, who fought from two-horse chariots that each carried a driver and a warrior. Shooting copper-headed arrows, chariot soldiers led the charge; they also fought with javelins and bronze swords. The chariotry was divided into a number of twenty-five-chariot squadrons,

each headed by an officer known as a Charioteer of the Residence.

Most of the army was made up of infantry, who fought on foot with bows and arrows, clubs, axes, slings, spears, swords, and daggers. When the Egyptian empire was not actively at war, soldiers manned fortresses in the conquered territories, making sure that they stayed conquered. Infantrymen may also have labored on public works projects in times of peace.

The infantry had several ranks of officers. The lowest of these was called the Greatest of Fifty, for he was in charge of fifty men; next came the standard bearer, who commanded two hundred. After three middle ranks came the overseer of garrison troops, whose superior was the overseer of fortresses. Above him was a lieutenant commander, who reported to the overseer of the army, also known as the Great Army General. The only step higher than this was the pharaoh himself. In fact, quite often the pharaoh appointed his chosen successor, the crown prince, to be Great Army General. This way, he would be prepared for his future role as commander in chief.

A nineteenth-century artist's copy of a relief from one of Ramses II's temples, showing the king leading his army against a Syrian city held by the Hittites

 FOUR

LADIES ROYAL AND NOBLE

any women were part of the pharaoh's court, including his chief wife, any sisters and daughters he might have, and his mother if she were still alive. Every pharaoh also supported numerous secondary wives. All of these women naturally had numbers of women attendants, too, and noblewomen probably joined their husbands at court functions from time to time.

A small group of women, including the pharaoh's chief wife, generally accompanied him on his travels in Egypt. Others lived together in various palace complexes throughout the country. The women always had their own quarters—even their own palaces— but they could come and go more or less as they pleased. The women's children also lived in these complexes (for convenience referred to as harems), and so did male administrators who managed the lands and businesses belonging to the palaces.

Opposite:
Nefertari, the chief queen of Ramses II, as portrayed in her tomb in the Valley of the Queens, roughly a mile south of the Valley of the Kings

31

THE KING'S GREAT WIFE

The two most powerful women in Egypt were the pharaoh's mother and his chief wife. We would refer to both these women as queens, but the ancient Egyptians were more specific. They used titles that meant "king's mother" and "king's great wife" or "great royal wife."

Many people believe that the great royal wife was always the king's sister, but this was not the case. When a king did marry his full or half sister, it was another way of setting himself apart from other Egyptians (who did not marry their siblings) and emphasizing the closeness between himself and the gods (who sometimes did). In addition, a brother-sister marriage kept royal privileges and wealth exclusively within the family. Moreover, this might be the only way for a pharaoh's daughter to have a husband of suitably high rank. As Amenhotep III answered the Babylonian king who asked to marry an Egyptian princess, "From time immemorial no daughter of the king of Egypt has been given in marriage to anyone."

Tiy, the great royal wife of Amenhotep III

Many great royal wives came from noble, but nonroyal, families. (This was the case with two of the most famous and influential queens of the New Kingdom: Tiy, married to Amenhotep III, and Nefertiti, married to their son Akhenaten.) Whether royal or noble in origin, the great royal wife became semidivine, like her husband. When a man was crowned pharaoh, one of the first things he usually did was name his great royal wife. It was essential to *maat* that he do so, because balance between male and female was one of the things that kept order in the universe.

We don't know as much as we would like about the activities of the king's great wife, but it seems clear that she was expected to accompany her husband in many of his duties and to stand by and show her support. For example, Thutmose III's principal queen, Merytre, was praised as "one who is never absent from the side of the Lord of the Two Lands." Many Egyptian works of art show the queen standing behind or beside the king during public appearances and religious ceremonies. The great royal wife played other religious roles. One of the titles she usually held was God's Wife of Amen, and often she was a priestess of the goddess Hathor, too.

The surviving evidence gives us hints of the respect and influence that at least some great royal wives enjoyed. We know that the position of God's Wife of Amen gave the queen title to lands and a portion of temple income, and authority over a large staff of male administrators and servants. In art, great royal wives were frequently shown wearing the distinctive headdresses of goddesses. Tiy was even portrayed on one monument as a sphinx trampling two female prisoners of war—a way of symbolizing the power over enemies that she shared with her husband. Tiy also engaged in diplomatic correspondence, as did Nefertari, Ramses II's queen. After Ramses made a peace treaty with Hatti, the powerful Hittite empire of Anatolia (modern-day Turkey), Nefertari wrote to the Hittite queen:

Nefertiti (*left*) with her daughters and husband, warmed by the rays of the sun god Aten

> With me, your sister, all goes well; with my country all
> goes well. With you, my sister, may all go well; with

your country may all go well. . . . May the sun god and storm god bring you joy; and may the sun god cause the peace to be good and give good brotherhood to the great king, the king of Egypt, with his brother the great king, the king of Hatti, forever. And I am in friendship and sisterly relations with my sister the great queen of Hatti, now and forever.

After the pharaoh died, the great royal wife might continue to exercise power and influence if her son succeeded to the throne. The king's mother, whether she had been great royal wife or not, was highly respected and could be a strong force in her son's rule. If the pharaoh came to the throne as a child, his mother could even govern the land as regent on his behalf.

THE WOMAN WHO WAS KING

As the daughter of Thutmose I and half sister and wife of Thutmose II, Hatshepsut bore the titles "King's Daughter, King's Sister, God's Wife and King's Great Wife." Hatshepsut had no son, so when her husband died, his young son by a secondary wife became pharaoh, Thutmose III. Hatshepsut governed Egypt as the boy-king's regent for several years, during which she gradually acquired more power. By the seventh year of Thutmose III's reign, she had become co-ruler, crowned as a pharaoh in her own right.

Hatshepsut was not the first woman to rule Egypt—there had been two or three before her, in the Old and Middle Kingdoms. But the "founding mothers" of the New Kingdom would have been much more familiar examples of powerful royal women. The first New Kingdom pharaoh, Ahmose, had a stela carved with an inscription that urged his subjects to honor his mother, Ahhotep, because "she has looked after her [that is, Egypt's] soldiers, she has guarded her, she has brought back her fugitives and collected together her deserters, she has pacified Upper Egypt and expelled her rebels." This sounds very much as though Ahhotep held the reins of government and commanded troops for a time, at least in the south—perhaps while Ahmose was still too young to rule, or while he was away fighting in northern Egypt. Ahmose's chief wife, Ahmose-Nefertari, was another strong woman, who held important priestly positions and sponsored the building of many monuments throughout Egypt. She even came to be worshipped as a goddess who watched over the Great Place.

No one knows exactly what led to Hatshepsut's becoming pharaoh, but she claimed authority as the daughter of both her earthly father, Thutmose I, and her divine father, Amen. One of her inscriptions says that Thutmose I proclaimed, "This daughter of mine . . . I have appointed as successor upon my throne. . . . It is she who will lead you. Obey her words and unite yourselves at her command." Amen was said to have planned to make Hatshepsut king even before her birth, and she in turn was enthusiastically devoted to him: "I am his daughter in very truth, who works for him and knows what he desires. My reward from my father is life, stability, dominion upon the Horus Throne of all the Living." To further reinforce her position and to show that she was upholding *maat* just like any other pharaoh, Hatshepsut had herself portrayed as a man in most of her official images, wearing the traditional kingly crown and false beard and performing traditional kingly tasks.

Hatshepsut wears the traditional false beard of Egyptian kings as she makes an offering to the gods.

Hatshepsut was on the throne for fifteen years (1473–1458 BCE), and this appears to have been a period of peace, prosperity, and good governance for Egypt. As we have already seen, Hatshepsut made important new additions to Amen's temple at Karnak, and she built or restored other temples as well. She also had a splendid mortuary temple built for herself near the entrance to the Great Place. This temple is known today as Deir el-Bahri; in ancient Egypt it was Djeser-Djeseru, "Holiest of the Holy." It is widely regarded as one of the most beautiful temples in all of Egypt.

Hatshepsut memorialized her reign in pictures and inscriptions on the walls of Djeser-Djeseru. The event she seems most proud of was an expedition to the land of Punt, somewhere in Africa near the southern end of the Red Sea. This was the climax of Hatshepsut's foreign policy of trade and exploration, which also included voyages to the eastern Mediterranean to obtain timber and the development of turquoise and copper mines in the Sinai Peninsula. The mission to Punt was led by Hatshepsut's chancellor, one of the most important men at court. He brought back to his pharaoh five shiploads of luxuries and marvels: frankincense, myrrh, incense trees, gold, semiprecious stones, ebony, leopard skins, elephant tusks, giraffes, monkeys, and cattle. "Never were brought such things to any king, since the world was," proclaimed the walls of Djeser-Djeseru.

LADIES OF RANK

After the great royal wife, the king's mother, and other female members of the royal family, the highest-ranking women in Egypt were his secondary wives. Many of them bore children to the pharaoh, and occasionally the son of a secondary wife became pharaoh himself—raising his mother to a position of the greatest importance. Even without this distinction, secondary

Sailors rowing a boat—one of the scenes of the expedition to Punt shown on the walls of Hatshepsut's temple

wives were highly respected. They were also busy. Their palaces or apartments were not only home to them and their children, but were also places of business and industry. Many harem-palaces had rights to land, its crops, and the labor of the peasants who lived on it. The royal ladies also trained women to weave fine linen and supervised large weaving workshops on the palace grounds.

During the New Kingdom, some secondary wives were daughters of foreign kings, sent to marry the pharaoh to cement peace treaties and alliances. Once the foreign women joined the harem, they were often given Egyptian names and might lose all contact with their own countries. For example, the king of Babylon wrote to Amenhotep III, "You are now asking for my daughter's hand in marriage, but my sister whom my father gave to you is already there with you, although no one has seen her or knows whether she is

THE MYSTERY OF NEFERTITI

One of the best-known Egyptian queens is Nefertiti, made famous by a beautiful bust of her that has been reproduced uncounted times in books and other media. Nefertiti, the great royal wife of Akhenaten (1352–1336 BCE), also seems to have been one of Egypt's most powerful queens. In art, she appears constantly with her husband, often accompanied by their daughters, in scenes of palace life and religious worship. She is also shown many times without her husband, which was quite unusual, and sometimes she was portrayed in ways that no (or very few) other queens were: driving a chariot, grasping enemies by the hair and preparing to club them on the head, enthroned while a group of foreign captives are paraded before her, rewarding men with gold, riding in a royal litter, and wearing crowns traditionally worn only by kings.

These images of Nefertiti have helped to convince some scholars that she was not just a powerful queen, but that she reigned alongside her husband as a full co-ruler. We may never know the truth of this, but one thing is clear: there are no images of Nefertiti or inscriptions mentioning her after the fourteenth year of Akhenaten's reign. The king had obviously been extremely devoted to his wife, so we would expect to find some mention of her death—if indeed she died at this time. If she didn't, did she go into retirement? One of her daughters had recently died, and perhaps the queen was so depressed that she withdrew from public life. Or was she in disgrace for some reason, and forced to withdraw? These are all possibilities that Egyptologists have considered.

Some scholars favor a much more radical explanation for Nefertiti's disappearance. They believe that Akhenaten made her not only his co-ruler but his official heir. In this new role, she took the throne name Smenkhkara. Indeed, this name first appears in the records at almost exactly the time that Nefertiti's vanishes. But two years later Akhenaten died, and Smenkhkara, too, disappeared. We do have a mummy identified as Smenkhkara's, but it is so damaged that it gives us little information. No tomb or mummy has ever been found for Nefertiti, and her fate may always remain a mystery.

A woman plays the double flute while her companions clap along. Careers in music were open to talented Egyptian women, who could work for noble families or for the temples.

alive or dead." On the other hand, these women did not leave their homelands alone: when Gilukhepa, a daughter of the king of Mitanni, went to Egypt to become yet another secondary wife of Amenhotep III, she brought with her an entourage of 317 women, all of whom entered the harem with her.

We know much less than we would like about the wives and daughters of noblemen and upper-level government officials. It is safe to say that aristocratic wives, just like queens, were expected to give their husbands unfailing support. These women also were responsible for the running of their homes. They did no housework themselves, of course, but they had many servants to supervise. If a noblewoman's husband was away at war or on some other duty for the pharaoh, then she would probably have to manage the family's business interests. Upper-class women were also very active in religion: we know of many examples of high-ranking ladies serving as singers and musicians in temples.

 **FIVE**

CHILDREN OF THE PALACE

lmost every ancient Egyptian, of whatever rank, wanted children—hopefully many of them. Being childless was one of the worst things that could happen to a married couple, and people used both medicines and magic to give them a better chance of having healthy babies. If nothing else worked, a childless couple might adopt an orphan or a younger child of a relative with a large family. For kings, with their many wives, this was not such a problem—Ramses II, for example, probably fathered well over a hundred children.

BIRTH AND CHILDHOOD

It seems that some babies, at least, were born in special structures known as birthing bowers, shelters set up outdoors, presumably in a courtyard or garden. Whether outdoors or in, however, babies were born at home. An upper-class woman was attended by one or

Opposite:
A woman carries her baby in a sling on her back while a slightly older child rides on her shoulders.

Midwives help a
woman give birth,
then the baby
nurses for the first
time as the deities
Amen and Mut
look on.

more midwives, probably with additional help from female relatives.

Even with the best assistance, many women and babies died during or soon after childbirth. The royal family itself was not immune from such tragedies. For example, one of Akhenaten's daughters died in childbirth, and tomb images show him and Nefertiti weeping over her body. Many Egyptologists believe that Akhenaten's favorite secondary wife, Lady Kiya, died giving birth to Tutankhamen. Later, Nefertiti's sister Mutnodjmet, the great royal wife of Horemheb (1323–1295), also died giving birth; the baby was either stillborn or died not long after its mother. The two were mummified and buried together.

When the mother died but the baby lived, another woman would nurse the child. Upper-class families often made use of wet nurses in any case. During the New Kingdom, wet-nursing was an honored job, and some of the most influential women in Egypt were the royal wet nurses. The position of royal wet nurse was so respected, in fact, that it was often held by the wives and mothers of the highest government officials.

Children were usually nursed for three years. They grew up in the women's quarters, where they were probably cared for not only by their own mothers or wet nurses but also, at times, by aunts, sisters, and other women. In artwork, children are usually shown naked; some of the time, they may have dressed in miniature versions of adult clothing. Upper-class children had their own distinctive hairstyle, called the "sidelock of youth": they were shaved bald except for a thick lock of hair on one side of the head. Amulets for magical protection were often braided into or hung from this sidelock.

Ramses III's son Amenherkhopeshef wears the "sidelock of youth" in this scene from his tomb. He died during childhood.

Children at court and in noble families had a variety of toys. There were dolls and doll cradles, puppets, toy animals, rattles, tops, and toy weapons. Some of the dolls and animals were made of wood and had movable parts. Others were made of clay. On the site of one harem-palace, archaeologists found several clay figures—including a crocodile, a pig, an ape, a hippopotamus, and a model boat—that looked as though they had been made by the children themselves.

Children also enjoyed a variety of games, including ball games and something resembling leapfrog. Boys seem to have been especially active: scenes on tomb walls show them racing, wrestling, tightrope walking, fishing, and target shooting. Many Egyptians of all ages were fond of pets: dogs (at least three different breeds), monkeys, geese, and especially cats. We know the name of at least one royal child's pet, Ta-Miu, meaning simply "The Cat."

THE PALACE SCHOOL

As children got older, they had less playtime: they had to be educated for their adult roles. A few girls, mostly king's daughters, learned to read and write, and perhaps to do basic math. Most girls, it seems, were mainly taught to weave and manage a household, even if in their adult life they would be supervising servants and not doing domestic tasks themselves. They might also learn some dancing and music, which would be especially useful if they took on religious duties later.

Royal boys, and the sons of many nobles, were taught in the palace school. Here they learned to read and write two forms of the Egyptian language: one using hieroglyphs, the other a simpler, cursive form. This scribal training was long and difficult. There were hundreds of different hieroglyphic signs, and teachers were known to beat lazy or reluctant pupils. Fortunately, more positive forms of encouragement were given, too; students were urged, "Emulate your fathers who were before you . . . See! their words are made lasting in writing."

The students practiced their writing skills on limestone flakes, pieces of broken pottery, or writing boards made from sycamore wood covered with a smooth layer of plaster. When they gained real skill at writing, they could use rolls of papyrus, paper made from reeds that grew in the swampy areas of the Nile Delta. The teacher dictated proverbs, bits of stories, and other material for the students to write out, or the students would make copies of selections from Egyptian literary classics and other texts. In the course of their copying and taking dictation, they would learn their country's history and literature. They also studied mathematics and other subjects that would enable them to become high-ranking government officials.

Military training, too, played an important part in the education

of well-born Egyptian boys, for many of them would be the army officers of the future. They learned archery, swordsmanship, and chariotry; they probably went on fairly regular hunting trips to hone these skills. Sometimes they even went to war with their fathers. When Ramses II, as crown prince, was sent to put down a rebellion in Nubia, he took along his two oldest sons, aged four and five.

The palace school was also attended by the sons of prominent families in the Asian territory under Egypt's control. These boys were basically hostages, insurance that people back home in western Asia wouldn't rebel against Egypt. Once the boys completed their education, they served the court as pages or guardsmen. After years of absorbing Egyptian values and living as Egyptians, they were finally sent back home to take their places as community leaders—leaders who would be dependably loyal to Egypt.

Boys work busily at their lessons. Each has a reed pen (with one end pounded or chewed to make a brush) and a palette, a piece of wood that holds two cakes of ink.

BECOMING AN ADULT

This life-size wooden mannequin, made to display clothes or jewelry, portrays the boy-king Tutankhamen.

There was no adolescence in ancient Egypt—you went straight from childhood to adulthood, usually in your early teens. For girls, this meant getting married, often to an older man. It was fairly common for girls to marry their uncles; first cousins often married, too. In the upper class, it seems that the two families concerned usually arranged the marriage, but love could also play a role. We even have at least one recorded instance of love at first sight: when the Hittite king sent his daughter to marry Ramses II, the pharaoh (according to stelae he had carved) took one look at her and saw that "she was beautiful in the opinion of His Majesty, and he loved her more than anything, as a momentous event for him." Even for royalty, however, there does not seem to have been any special wedding ceremony; once the couple was living together, they were considered married.

Boys might wait a little longer than girls to marry, as they finished their educations and started "on-the-job" training in their careers. Ramses II spent much of his teenage years overseeing the quarrying of granite for royal monuments on behalf of his father, Seti I. In addition, he accompanied Seti to war at the age of about fourteen and took part in military campaigns under supervision until he was twenty-two, when he had his first solo command. By this time, Ramses had been married for roughly seven years and already had several children of his own.

Some royal boys found themselves in positions of power even before they left childhood. The most famous boy-king is of course Tutankhamen, whose almost-untouched tomb was discovered in 1922, full of fabulous objects. Tutankhamen was probably about nine when he became king. Nine years later, he was dead. Even for royal children, life could be all too brief.

 SIX

PASTIMES AND FESTIVITIES

gypt's upper class was comprised of just a few hundred families, who enjoyed wealth and privileges far out of the reach of the common people. One privilege, much celebrated in the texts copied out by students, was that well-born and well-educated Egyptians did not have to do manual labor. "Be a scribe [an educated man] that your limbs may be sleek, . . . that you may not be extinguished like a lamp," says one ancient author. Another asserts, "As for the scribe, no matter what position he finds himself in the (royal) Residence, he will not be uncomfortable in it." Naturally, the higher position a man and his family obtained at court, the more comfort they could enjoy.

LEISURE TIME

The upper-class lifestyle gave plenty of opportunities for relaxation and recreation. Games of all kinds were very popular, and

Opposite:
Queen Nefertari plays *senet*, a board game that may have been a bit like Parcheesi.

some of the world's earliest board games come from Egypt. The favorite among rulers and nobles was probably *senet*. This was a game for two players, each of whom had five to seven pieces to move. The board had thirty squares, in three rows of ten each, and players determined their moves by tossing four sticks. The goal apparently was to be the first one to get all your game pieces to the square marked with the hieroglyph meaning "happiness and beauty."

Banqueting was one of the best-loved forms of recreation for upper-class Egyptians, who enjoyed both giving and attending parties. Diners sat at small tables, two people to each, and ate with their hands. Servants brought around trays of food, and the guests selected whatever looked good to them. Flowers were everywhere, decorating the tables, the guests, and even the wine jars.

We can begin to get a picture of what was involved in a royal or noble host's banquet from this ancient list of party preparations:

> Have made 200 ring-stands for bouquets of flowers, 500 food-baskets. Foodstuff list, to be prepared: 1,000 loaves of fine flour, 10,000 *ibshet*-biscuits, 2,000 *tjet*-loaves; cakes, 100 baskets; dried meat, 100 baskets of 300 cuts; milk, 60 measures; cream, 90 measures; carob-beans, 30 bowls. Grapes, 50 sacks; pomegranates, 60 sacks; figs, 300 strings and 20 baskets.

In addition to the foods just mentioned, well-off Egyptians enjoyed dates, melons, leeks, onions, garlic, celery, cucumbers, radishes, and romaine lettuce. Meats included duck, goose, beef, and mutton. We don't have any ancient Egyptian recipes, unfortunately, but we do know that foods were sometimes prepared with olive oil and flavored with herbs such as mint, marjoram, dill, cumin, coriander, and cilantro; sweetness was provided by dates or honey. The favorite drink was wine.

Entertainment was an important part of the banqueting experience. It just wasn't a party without musicians, singers, dancers, and acrobats. Most of these entertainers were women. Often there was also a man playing the harp. He might sing a song like this one:

> Follow your desire,
> allow the heart to forget . . .
> Dress yourself in garments of fine linen . . .
> Increase your beauty,
> and let not your heart languish.
> Follow your desire and what is good.
> Conduct yourself on earth
> after the dictates of your heart—
> Celebrate
> but tire not yourself with it.
> Remember, no man takes his goods with him,
> and none have returned after going!

A blind harpist, sitting cross-legged on the floor, sings to entertain banquet guests.

Some entertainers came to Egypt as prisoners of war from western Asia. One pharaoh, reporting on the results of a military campaign, bragged that he had captured and brought back 270 musicians.

ACTIVE PURSUITS

Upper-class men, especially when they were young, were often very athletic. They enjoyed wrestling, horse training, chariot driving, archery, and javelin throwing. These activities all had the added benefit of keeping the men in training for warfare. The upper classes

This woman, carrying bunches of grapes at a banquet, wears typical Egyptian eyeliner.

THE ART OF LOOKING GOOD

Upper-class Egyptians spent some of their free time caring for their personal appearance. Being clean, well dressed, and well made-up was a pleasure in its own right for many men and women, but it was also a sign of wealth and high status.

The Egyptians didn't have soap as we know it. They cleansed themselves with natron, a kind of salt. Natron was very drying, so after bathing, the wealthy rubbed perfumed oils or lotions into their skin; this also gave them some protection against the harsh Egyptian sun and wind. For protection against body odor, they used a deodorant made from powdered carob beans or a mixture of incense and porridge. To sweeten the breath, women in particular were advised to chew small pills made of frankincense, myrrh, and cinnamon.

The clothes of the well-to-do were made of fine linen, sun-bleached white; the garments were distinguished by their many pleats. Women of the New Kingdom usually wore a long, flowing robe. Men might wear a similar style, especially for festive occasions, or they wore a knee-length kilt. Color was added to these outfits mainly by jewelry made of gold and semiprecious stones. Some pieces of jewelry may have been purely decorative, but others had religious meaning or were forms of magical protection. For men, a certain kind of gold collar, awarded by the pharaoh, was a mark of loyal government service. Men who had served the king well were also entitled to wear earrings.

Both men and women wore wigs and makeup. For comfort in Egypt's hot climate, many people shaved their heads or cut their hair very short. Wigs then allowed them to still wear elaborate hairstyles on special occasions. When the temperature cooled at night, a wig also kept a person's head warm. Makeup served a similar dual purpose. Well-off Egyptians liked the look of their elaborate eye makeup, made from ground-up minerals—malachite for green and galena for dark gray—mixed with ointment. They also felt that the thick eyeliner helped protect their eyes from the glaring sun and wind-borne sand that were constant features of Egyptian life.

A mirror made of polished metal that belonged to Queen Ahhotep. The Egyptian word for *mirror* literally meant "see-face."

also liked to watch athletic competitions, such as wrestling matches, archery contests, and stick-fencing.

One of the most popular activities was hunting. Some pharaohs boasted as proudly about their exploits on the hunt as about their achievements on the battlefield. In the second year of his reign, Amenhotep III had a large scarab carved to proclaim his prowess:

> His Majesty was informed "There are wild bulls in the desert. . . ." Then His Majesty appeared upon his chariot, the entire army behind him, the officers and men of the whole army and the young men with them were commanded to watch over the wild bulls. Then His Majesty gave orders that the bulls be rounded up into an enclosure with a ditch. Then His Majesty rode out against these wild bulls. . . . The total which His Majesty took on the hunt on this day—fifty-six bulls. His Majesty waited four days to give rest to his horses and then His Majesty appeared again on his chariot. The number of bulls which he took on the hunt— forty wild bulls.

Later Amenhotep issued a scarab proclaiming that in the first ten years of his reign he killed 102 lions. Pharaohs also enjoyed hunting ostriches, gazelles, and ibex in the Egyptian desert, and elephants in Syria. When kings weren't hunting animals, they often collected them, turning part of the palace grounds into a kind of zoo. Thutmose III's collection included exotic plants and birds as well as elephants, bears, rhinoceroses, and other animals.

As Amenhotep III's scarab indicates, the royal big-game hunts were grand affairs in which the king might be joined by many nobles. Hunting small animals, on the other hand, was often the

occasion for a family outing. Many paintings have survived that show an upper-class man out on a little boat made of bundled papyrus reeds, duck hunting in marshy areas of the Nile. His wife stands by, watching, as he raises his throw stick to bring down a bird. At least one of his children crouches beside him in the boat; sometimes the children entertain themselves by picking the lotus flowers that grow in the water. The family cat may even be along for the day, helping out by retrieving the downed waterfowl.

Sightseeing was another kind of outing that many Egyptians enjoyed. The biggest "tourist attraction" was the Great Pyramid of Giza (together with the surrounding pyramids), which was close to a thousand years old by the time of the New Kingdom pharaohs. For many people, these visits to ancient sites were, at least in part, religious experiences. Around 1200 BCE, a man named Hednakht left graffiti on the Step Pyramid of Saqqara asking the gods to give him "a full lifetime in serving your good pleasure" and "a goodly burial after a happy old age." Prince Kaemwaset, the fourth son of Ramses II, took an even more active interest in historic sites. He

Nakht (shown twice), a scribe in the service of Thutmose IV, enjoys some time hunting in the marshes with his family. The children seem eager to try out their own throw sticks.

inspected and restored many of the monuments of the past, inspired, as he said, by his "love for the ancient days" and for "the perfection of all that his ancestors achieved."

A ROYAL CELEBRATION

The Egyptians observed many holidays throughout the year. One occasion, however, was so special that it was only supposed to be celebrated after the pharaoh had been on the throne for thirty years. This festival was called the *heb-sed*, often translated as "jubilee." Its purpose was to honor the stability of the pharaoh's long reign and to renew his strength so that he could continue to be strong in upholding *maat*.

Some pharaohs did not wait the full thirty years to celebrate their jubilee, and some held more than one. Akhenaten's *heb-sed*, for example, took place only four years after his coronation. Ramses II followed tradition and celebrated his first *heb-sed* in the thirtieth year of his reign. He was fifty-five at the time and, amazingly, he went on to rule for another thirty-six years. During those years he must have felt the need for renewal repeatedly, because he held an additional twelve jubilees.

Kings often spent months or even years preparing for the *heb-sed*. Many ordered the construction of new monuments to commemorate the jubilee—Hatshepsut's second pair of obelisks, for instance, were erected on the occasion of her *heb-sed*. The

Nobles gathered for a festive occasion sniff lotus flowers as they enjoy the entertainment of musicians and dancers.

pharaohs also had special facilities constructed for the celebration of the jubilee itself. Amenhotep III ordered the building of a whole complex, including a brightly painted festival hall and a huge artificial lake.

When everything was at last prepared, the *heb-sed* began with a proclamation on the anniversary of the pharaoh's accession to the throne. Many days of festivity followed, ending with a magnificent procession of statues of the gods and goddesses. Queen Tiy's steward, Kheruef, organized Amenhotep III's first *heb-sed*; he had pictures and descriptions of some of the highlights recorded on his tomb walls:

> The glorious appearance of the King at the great double doors in his palace, "The House of Rejoicing"; ushering in the officials, the king's friends, the chamberlain, the men of the gateway, the king's acquaintances . . . Rewards were given out in the form of "Gold of Praise" and golden ducks and fish, and they received ribbons of green linen, each person being made to stand in order of rank.

In addition to the distribution of rewards for faithful service, the jubilee included solemn rites, such as a reenactment of the coronation. There was also a ceremonial race in which the king, carrying royal emblems, ran around the festival pavilion four times to prove his strength. Naturally, there were also banquets and other special events. These took place all over the country, with the king making visits throughout the realm; the entire celebration could go on for months. The *heb-sed* probably gave the Egyptian people a feeling of reassurance and renewed confidence in their ruler. In addition, everyone appreciated the feasting, entertainment, and days off work that went along with the national celebration.

SEVEN

PALACE PROBLEMS

he images and inscriptions on tomb walls and monuments can give us the impression that ancient Egypt was a land of few troubles, where everyone lived a pleasant, well-ordered life. This is the impression that the pharaohs and nobles wanted to give. Tombs and monuments existed largely to make certain that a person remained alive in memory after death—and everyone wanted their lives and their deeds to be remembered well. But other kinds of records, combined with the evidence of the mummies that were buried in the tombs, give us a picture of some of the more unpleasant realities of life in ancient Egypt.

HEALTH HAZARDS

The Egyptians possessed the most advanced medical knowledge and techniques in the ancient world. They knew, for example, that something in bread mold (the original source of antibiotics) could

Opposite:
A bronze sculpture of a sick man, barely able to endure the pain of his illness

keep wounds from becoming infected. They used needles to stitch wounds closed, and they used sharp knives to perform many kinds of surgery. But even so, and even though upper-class Egyptians had the best access to medical care, disease and injury caused suffering and death to many.

We have already seen how dangerous childbirth was for both mothers and babies. Part of the reason was that girls married so young—too often their bodies simply weren't mature enough for pregnancy and birth. The young were also especially vulnerable to disease; two or three of Akhenaten's daughters, for example, seem to have died during an epidemic of the plague. If a person survived childhood, though, there was a good chance of living to be forty or so. Some well-off Egyptians, thanks to the advantages they had in food and housing and so on, survived into their fifties or sixties. A few remarkable people even lived to be seventy or eighty, and Ramses II was ninety when he died.

The older people got, however, the more health problems they were likely to have. Arthritis was one of the most common afflictions, and the swellings at the joints on some mummies show that during life, these people must have suffered a great deal of pain. The other major health hazard was dental disease. Doctors coped with it as best they could, and surviving papyrus scrolls contain many recipes for dental treatments. One reads, "To treat a tooth which is eaten away where the gums begin: cumin, frankincense and carob pulp are powdered and applied to the tooth."

Too often, it was a losing battle. Egyptians of all classes ate large amounts of bread, which was made from stone-ground flour. Moreover, it was impossible to keep sand out of the flour. So between the sand and bits of stone, over the years eating bread wore away the outer layers of the teeth, making them highly vulnerable to bacteria. Abcessed teeth caused great pain even to members of the royal household, and these infections led to death in many cases.

And then there were a wide variety of parasites to contend with. Upper-class advantages gave some protection from parasitic infections. For example, wealthy people generally plucked or shaved off all their body hair, which helped keep disease-carrying lice and fleas off them. The higher class also enjoyed better sanitary conditions than the majority of Egyptians. Nevertheless, many parasites lived in the waters of the Nile, and very few people could fail to come into contact with them. Some could cause serious damage to the body's tissues, which might result in a variety of unpleasant conditions and even in death.

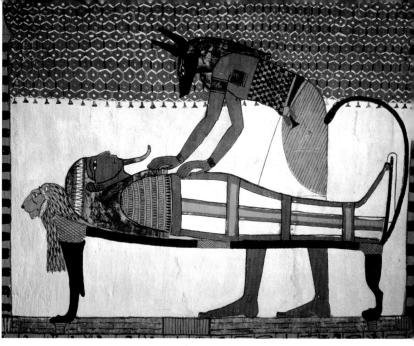

Anubis, the god who presided over funerals, bends over the mummy of an official.

In the 1970s and again in the 1990s, scientists studied the mummy of a New Kingdom lady named Asru. They wanted to get a better idea of what sort of health problems affected the ancient Egyptians. Asru was probably in her fifties when she died, and arthritis afflicted her finger joints and her knees. At some point she had suffered an injury to her lower back, resulting in pressure on her spinal cord which must have caused continual pain in her back and legs. She was missing many of her back teeth and had endured a major infection in her jaw; she probably lived with toothaches more or less constantly. She had had at least three parasitic infections. One had damaged her lungs so that she must have had difficulty breathing, and the others appeared to have caused anemia and persistent diarrhea. Asru had enjoyed a privileged lifestyle, but still she suffered most of the health problems common to her time.

ENEMIES OF THE CROWN

The New Kingdom began in battle and strife, and pharaohs continued to go to war frequently to enforce loyalty in conquered territories. At home, however, Egypt enjoyed long periods of peace and prosperity. The first threat to this happy state came during the reign of Akhenaten (1352–1336). He broke with many of Egypt's time-honored traditions: he favored the god Aten over Amen and all the other deities, and he moved his capital to a brand-new city, built to his own specifications. Once settled there, he never left, and he seems to have neglected many of his government duties.

The Hittite empire was gaining strength at this time, and Hittite forces were marching on Egyptian-held territory in Syria. The local rulers pleaded with Akhenaten for protection: "They say that the king my lord will not march out. So let my lord dispatch archers, and let them come." The pharaoh apparently ignored these pleas, and much of Syria fell to the invaders. It was left to Akhenaten's successors to beat back the Hittites and reclaim the northern part of the Egyptian empire. To these successors, Akhenaten would always be known as "the enemy," a king who had failed to uphold *maat*.

Prisoners, still wearing their distinctive feathered headdresses, captured during Ramses III's war against the Sea Peoples

The next great threat came during the reign of Ramses III (1184–1153). Libyans, from west of Egypt, tried to invade the Nile Delta. No sooner had Ramses driven them out than he had even worse problems. The whole eastern Mediterranean was being harassed by a loose-knit confederation known as the Sea Peoples. Many of them were seafarers who seem to have come from Greece and the nearby islands. Others were nomads and farmers who traveled by land, whole families migrating with all their possessions.

The Sea Peoples overthrew the Hittite Empire, then attacked Syria. As they moved closer to Egypt, the Egyptian navy went out to meet their ships. Ramses' archers mowed down the invaders, and when the battle was over, the Sea Peoples could no longer threaten Egypt. But the Libyans still could, and Ramses was soon at war again. After yet another victory, it seemed that all would at last be well. But as Ramses neared the end of his thirty-first year as pharaoh, the unthinkable happened: someone dared to plot against the pharaoh.

The office of pharaoh was sacred—once the king was crowned, he was more than human. He was the divinely endowed upholder of *maat*, and to try to harm or overthrow him would invite the forces of chaos to take hold of Egypt. But now Tiye, one of Ramses III's secondary wives, launched a conspiracy to kill him and put her son on the throne. Forty people became involved in Tiye's plan, and their strategy even included stealing a book of royal magic so that they could use forbidden spells to overcome the palace guard. The conspiracy was discovered, and most of the plotters were executed or forced to commit suicide. But Ramses died anyway, perhaps even before the sentences were carried out.

After this, Egypt did indeed fall into chaos. The New Kingdom lasted another eighty or so years, but they were years of trouble and disunity. By the end of this period, the empire was lost and Egypt was once more divided, the north and south basically two separate countries.

Egyptian art, like this serene portrait of a royal Egyptian, focused on the ideal, but other sources have revealed that even for royalty life was often less than perfect.

The most glorious era of Egyptian history was gone—but never quite forgotten. In the following centuries, Egyptian kings looked back to Thutmose III and the other great New Kingdom rulers as honored ancestors and role models. And today, thanks to the discoveries and studies of Egyptologists, the life of ancient Egypt becomes ever more vivid to us. The Egyptians believed that so long as a pharaoh's name was kept alive, where people could see it carved into enduring stone, the pharaoh's spirit, too, would stay alive among the immortal gods. We can see, appreciate, and celebrate the spirit of all the Egyptian people as we read about them and admire their art and monuments. And Egypt's immortal achievements can inspire us to dream big, to celebrate life and beauty, and perhaps even to find and uphold our own version of *maat*.

GLOSSARY

alabaster a soft, translucent milky-white stone often carved into vases, cosmetic jars, and lamps

dynasty a series of rulers who were usually related by family ties

ebony a hard, black wood; when it is highly polished, it shines almost like metal

electrum a mixture of silver and gold

harem the private apartments or palaces where the pharaohs' wives and children lived

hieroglyph a stylized picture that stood for a word, concept, group of consonants, or single consonant

Horus a falcon-headed god who was especially concerned with the rulers of Egypt. The king was often said to be the Living Horus, and his divine authority could be symbolized by the Horus Throne.

inscription words written on or carved into lasting materials such as stone or metal

pharaoh an ancient Egyptian king (or, occasionally, queen). The title *pharaoh*—or, in its original form, *per aa*—for an Egyptian ruler came into use during the New Kingdom. It initially meant "great house" and referred to the royal palace. (Compare this to the way we sometimes say "the White House" to mean the president.)

pylon two towers, wider at the bottom than at the top, connected in the middle to make a huge ceremonial gateway

scarab a kind of beetle, or a stone or other object made in the shape of a scarab beetle

scribe a man who made his living by reading and writing. In a broader sense, the ancient Egyptians used *scribe* to mean an educated man, one who did not have to do manual labor but was qualified to serve in government or temple administration. A scribal education was so valued

that even the highest nobles and officials proudly referred to themselves as scribes.

stela a stone slab or plaque carved with words and/or images to commemorate an important person or event. The plural is *stelae*.

throne name the name by which a pharaoh was most commonly known after his coronation. Today we usually refer to pharaohs by their birth names, but when they were crowned they took four additional names, including the throne name.

vizier the most powerful government official next to the king; a kind of prime minister. The ancient Egyptian term for this office was *tjaty*.

FOR FURTHER READING

Berger, Melvin, and Gilda Berger. *Mummies of the Pharaohs: Exploring the Valley of the Kings.* Washington, DC: National Geographic, 2001.

Caselli, Giovanni. *In Search of Tutankhamun: The Discovery of a King's Tomb.* New York: Peter Bedrick, 2001.

Chrisp, Peter. *Ancient Egypt Revealed.* New York: Dorling Kindersley, 2002.

Douglas, Vincent, et al. *Illustrated Encyclopedia of Ancient Egypt.* New York: Peter Bedrick, 2001.

Green, Roger Lancelyn. *Tales of Ancient Egypt.* New York: Puffin Books, 1956 (reissued 2004).

Greenblatt, Miriam. *Hatshepsut and Ancient Egypt.* New York: Benchmark Books, 2000.

Harris, Nathaniel. *Everyday Life in Ancient Egypt.* New York: Franklin Watts, 1994.

Hart, George. *Ancient Egypt.* New York: Dorling Kindersley, 2000.

Hawass, Zahi. *Curse of the Pharaohs: My Adventures with Mummies.* Washington, DC: National Geographic, 2004.

Jovinelly, Joann, and Jason Netelkos. *The Crafts and Culture of the Ancient Egyptians.* New York: Rosen Publishing Group, 2002.

Manning, Ruth. *Ancient Egyptian Women.* Chicago: Heinemann Library, 2002.

Marston, Elsa. *The Ancient Egyptians.* New York: Benchmark Books, 1996.

Millard, Anne. *The Pharaoh.* New York: Peter Bedrick, 2001.

Perl, Lila. *The Ancient Egyptians*. Danbury, CT: Franklin Watts, 2004.

Streissguth, Thomas. *Life in Ancient Egypt*. San Diego: Lucent Books, 2001.

Tames, Richard. *Ancient Egyptian Children*. Chicago: Heinemann Library, 2002.

ONLINE INFORMATION*

Akhet Egyptology: The Horizon to the Past.
   http://www.akhet.co.uk/

The British Museum. *Ancient Egypt*.
   http://www.ancientegypt.co.uk/menu.html

Civilization.ca. *Mysteries of Egypt: Tutankhamun*.
   http://www.civilization.ca/civil/egypt/egtut01e.html

Kinnaer, Jacques. *The Ancient Egypt Site*.
   http://www.ancient-egypt.org/

Metropolitan Museum of Art. *The Art of Ancient Egypt: A Web Resource*.
   http://www.metmuseum.org/explore/newegypt/htm/a_index.htm

Museum of Fine Arts. *Explore Ancient Egypt*.
   http://www.mfa.org/egypt/explore_ancient_egypt/

Nova Online. *Secrets of Lost Empires: Pharaoh's Obelisk*.
   http://www.pbs.org/wgbh/nova/lostempires/obelisk/

Odyssey Online. *Egypt*.
   http://www.carlos.emory.edu/ODYSSEY/EGYPT/homepg.html

*All Internet sites were available and accurate when this book was sent to press.

BIBLIOGRAPHY

Clayton, Peter A. *Chronicle of the Pharaohs: The Reign-by-Reign Record of the Rulers and Dynasties of Ancient Egypt*. New York: Thames and Hudson, 1994.

David, Rosalie. *Handbook to Life in Ancient Egypt*. New York: Facts on File, 1998.

Editors of Time-Life Books. *Egypt: Land of the Pharaohs*. Alexandria, VA: Time-Life Books, 1992.

———. *Ramses II: Magnificence on the Nile*. Alexandria, VA: Time-Life Books, 1993.

El Mahdy, Christine. *Tutankhamen: The Life and Death of the Boy-King*. New York: St. Martin's Press, 1999.

Fagan, Brian. *Egypt of the Pharaohs*. Washington: National Geographic, 2001.

James, Peter, and Nick Thorpe. *Ancient Inventions*. New York: Ballantine Books, 1994.

James, T. G. H. *Pharaoh's People: Scenes from Life in Imperial Egypt.* New York: Tauris Parke Paperbacks, 2003.

Mertz, Barbara. *Red Land, Black Land: Daily Life in Ancient Egypt.* rev. ed. New York: Dodd, Mead, 1978.

———. *Temples, Tombs and Hieroglyphs: A Popular History of Ancient Egypt.* rev. ed. New York: Peter Bedrick Books, 1978.

Romer, John. *Ancient Lives: Daily Life in Egypt of the Pharaohs.* New York: Henry Holt, 1984.

Shaw, Ian, ed. *The Oxford History of Ancient Egypt.* Oxford: Oxford University Press, 2000.

Silverman, David P., ed. *Ancient Egypt.* New York: Oxford University Press, 1997.

Trigger, B. G., et al. *Ancient Egypt: A Social History.* Cambridge: Cambridge University Press, 1983.

Tyldesley, Joyce. *Daughters of Isis: Women of Ancient Egypt.* New York: Penguin Books, 1995.

———. *Hatchepsut: The Female Pharaoh.* New York: Penguin Books, 1996.

———. *Judgement of the Pharaoh: Crime and Punishment in Ancient Egypt.* London: Weidenfeld and Nicolson, 2000.

———. *Nefertiti: Egypt's Sun Queen.* New York: Viking, 1998.

———. *The Private Lives of the Pharaohs.* New York: TV Books, 2000.

SOURCES FOR QUOTATIONS

This series of books tries to bring the ancient Egyptians to life by quoting their own words whenever possible. The quotations in this book are from the following sources:

Chapter 1: A God on Earth

p. 2 "all that the sun": Silverman, *Ancient Egypt,* p. 50.

p. 3 "His majesty became enraged": Fagan, *Egypt of the Pharaohs,* p. 184.

p. 3 "fled headlong to Megiddo": Mertz, *Temples, Tombs and Hieroglyphs,* p. 184.

p. 5 "Then my Majesty gave": ibid., p. 185.

p. 7 "Act justly": James, *Pharaoh's People,* p. 73.

Chapter 2: Building for This Life and the Next

p. 16 "He relaxed in the shadow": El Mahdy, *Tutankhamen,* p. 325.

p. 19 "supervised the excavation": Tyldesley, *Hatchepsut,* p. 71.

p. 19 "a fortress made out of": Tyldesley, *Nefertiti,* p. 18.

Chapter 3: Men of Influence

p. 22 "I judged both": James, *Pharaoh's People,* p. 57.

p. 22 "See to the office": ibid., p. 59.

p. 22 "See equally the man": ibid., p. 61.

p. 23 "a hall with records": ibid., p. 61.

p. 23 "Do not act": ibid., p. 61.

p. 24 "It is he": ibid., p. 66.

p. 25 "multitudes of workmen": Fagan, *Egypt of the Pharaohs*, p. 242.

p. 27 "I was a favourite": Clayton, *Chronicle of the Pharaohs*, p. 102.

p. 27 "Her Majesty praised": Tyldesley, *Hatchepsut*, p. 116.

p. 27 "I recorded the victories": Clayton, *Chronicle of the Pharaohs*, p. 109.

p. 28 "the Hereditary Prince": El Mahdi, *Tutankhamen*, p. 157.

Chapter 4: Ladies Royal and Noble

p. 32 "From time immemorial": Tyldesley, *Nefertiti*, p. 28.

p. 33 "one who is never": Tyldesley, *Daughters of Isis*, p. 192.

p. 33 "With me, your sister": Editors of Time-Life, *Ramses II*, pp. 90–91.

p. 34 "King's Daughter": Tyldesley, *Daughters of Isis*, p. 222.

p. 34 "she has looked after": Tyldesley, *Hatchepsut*, p. 57.

p. 35 "This daughter of mine": Tyldesley, *Daughters of Isis*, p. 226.

p. 35 "I am his daughter": Tyldesley, *Hatchepsut*, p. 154.

p. 36 "Never were brought": ibid., p. 151.

p. 37 "You are now asking": Tyldesley, *Nefertiti*, p. 28.

Chapter 5: Children of the Palace

p. 44 "Emulate your fathers": James, *Pharaoh's People*, p. 138.

p. 46 "she was beautiful": Editors of Time-Life, *Ramses II*, p. 87.

Chapter 6: Pastimes and Festivities

p. 49 "Be a scribe": James, *Pharaoh's People*, p. 143.

p. 49 "As for the scribe": ibid., p. 147.

p. 50 "Have made 200": Editors of Time-Life, *Ramses II*, pp. 95–96.

p. 51 "Follow your desire": Romer, *Ancient Lives*, p. 53.

p. 54 "His Majesty was informed": El Mahdi, *Tutankhamen*, pp. 320–321.

p. 55 "a full lifetime" and "a goodly burial": Editors of Time-Life, *Egypt*, p. 46.

p. 56 "love for" and "the perfection": ibid., p. 47.

p. 57 "The glorious appearance": Tyldesley, *Nefertiti*, p. 31.

Chapter 7: Palace Problems

p. 60 "To treat a tooth": Tyldesley, *The Private Lives of the Pharaohs*, p. 179.

p. 62 "They say that the king": Editors of Time-Life, *Egypt*, p. 101.

INDEX

ABOUT THE AUTHOR

When Kathryn Hinds was in sixth grade, she wanted to be an Egyptologist more than anything. Eventually she discovered that her true calling was writing, but she still loves archaeology and ancient history. She has written a number of books for young people about premodern cultures, including the books in the series LIFE IN THE ROMAN EMPIRE, LIFE IN THE RENAISSANCE, and LIFE IN THE MIDDLE AGES. Kathryn lives in the north Georgia mountains with her husband, their son, and an assortment of cats and dogs. When she is not writing, she enjoys spending time with her family and friends, reading, dancing, playing music, gardening, knitting, and taking walks in the woods.

Fox Gradin, Celestial Studios Photography